To Bend and Braid

To Bend and Braid

poems by

Emily Patterson

Cover design by Shay Culligan
Cover image by Annie Spratt
Author photo by Devon Albeit

ISBN: 978-1-63980-374-3

Kelsay Books
502 South 1040 East, A-119
American Fork, Utah 84003
Kelsaybooks.com

for Saoirse

&

for B.

Acknowledgments

Gratitude is given to the publications below, where many of these poems first appeared, sometimes in earlier forms:

A-Minor Magazine: "Wean, or One Afternoon My Breast Blooms Bright as a Poppy—"

Duck Head Journal: "Party Dress"

Minerva Rising Press: "Blank Slate," "On the Playground, I Think about How a Mother Is Like a Moth" (nominated for the Pushcart Prize, 2021), "Tomato Season"

Nightingale & Sparrow: "In Walhalla Ravine,"

Oyster River Pages: "Fiddleheads, or When My Hair Began to Grow Back"

Rust & Moth: "Aubade at Clear Creek"

Sapling (Quillkeepers Press): "To My Daughter at the Park in Late Spring"

Sheila-Na-Gig online: "To My Daughter in the Living Room, Dancing," "Womb"

Sky Island Journal: "Lungs, or Inside the Winter White We Fold," "Whether Trees Have Bones"

Spry Literary Journal: "Meeting Great Grandad After Lockdown"

SWWIM Every Day: "Light Feast on the Olentangy"

Trees, Seas & Attitude: An Anthology of Competition Entries (The Black Cat Poetry Press): "Whether Trees Have Bones"

Contents

Fiddleheads,
or When My Hair Began to Grow Back

Some of your hair is longer now
than some of mine: the nut-brown

curls at the back of your neck
mirroring the short spirals

that frame my face like
fiddleheads. Once I walked

four miles of forest
with you within me, tiny

green scrolls stretching
upward and everywhere;

not knowing, then, that they were
ferns still furled into themselves,

so new to this world—not knowing
that if left to grow, they would soon

transform to crimped triangles,
a coolness in their wake,

their presence like water
or the memory of it.

Womb

That night in Boulder you woke up
by the hour, the mountain air searing
a nasal edge into your cries. I held you

as you drifted into another brief span
of sleep—my own eyes full of sand,
my own heart working hard beneath

the Flatirons—until sometime around
three, when I turned on the shower,
took you into the steam that fogged

the mirror and blurred our reflections
in the half-dark. I held you as we pulled
the water-laden air into our mouths,

our bellies—leaning into its familiar
weight, the kind we were used to,
the kind we both knew from our

mothers' bodies, our earliest nights.

To My Daughter at the Park in Late Spring

You collect whirlers from the maple tree,
plucking their wings to pieces
to reveal the waxy seed.

I am learning to be at constant attention:
ready to sweep your hand from your mouth
in one swift motion.

I am learning, too, that sometimes the strip
of grass inside your cheek isn't worth it
for either of us.

Weeks ago, you would have sat contentedly
on this soft quilt, singing to the seeds,
glancing at me on occasion.

Now all you see is an ocean of green
and you glide to it, knowing exactly
what you seek in this world.

Now I realize it's me who lags:
still learning to keep pace
with your wonder.

On the Playground, I Think about How a Mother Is Like a Moth

In this bright world of play—
all blues and greens, the creak

      of swings—your laugh alights
      like dandelion seeds.

Folding your fingers
around mine, you slide

      down from the plastic perch
      with one brief shriek,

then motion for more:
again, again.

      Soon, you'll roam this place
      on your own, seek

my hands some other way,
or not at all.

      Above us in an ancient oak,
      there is a sun-bleached

kite, wings worn soft
as a moth's—

      a creature caught,
      yet willingly tethered.

Anniversary at New River

From up here, I said, *the trees look like*
one kind of tree. But we know better

now, which is why we can't stay here,
up on Diamond Outlook above

the grey-white water dotted with
miniature kayaks, a state away

from our one-year-old daughter.
We'll have to wade back in,

back down where there is space
between the roots, both needles

and leaves and occasional petals,
clear pebbles mired in mud—

I could go on. *But isn't it amazing,*
how all the way up here,

we can still hear the rapids
calling our names?

Tomato Season

We wander rows and point to seedlings,
leafy and lush: *Adoration, Early Girl, Fourth*

of July. Each one promising bright globes,
sun-ripened and sweet, a whole summer

to reap. This is your second tomato
season. Last year, I ate Sun Golds

by the handful, straight from the vine,
bare feet swollen in the soft soil; later,

I filled bowls with you tied to my chest,
asleep in evening light. At the nursery,

we arrange our new plants on a cart,
coupled with peppers and melons;

beaming, you pluck a spiny leaf,
bring it to your mouth—

as if you already know
that these fruits, you will taste.

Fairytale

As you pull books from the shelf
with reckless joy—pages

      revealing unruly kingdoms,
      a beast with wings,

mermaids in midnight
waters—I try to smile,

      to put them back
      in their places unnoticed,

turning from you only briefly,
but then you are gone.

      My whole body quickens
      with wordless terror,

my mind grows wild
as forest, shadowed

      and unknown—until
      I find you grinning

between the shelves,
unaware of your own

      absence, the momentary dark
      I tell myself is only

fiction, yet leaves me
blinking into the light

      for hours.

As You Continue Singing

You spear pasta spirals
with a pink plastic fork,

your movements both
determined and entirely

ineffective, and although
you sing softly, sweetly,

it's an exercise I find
hard to watch. I try

to read—peeking over
the pages, putting on

patience—when I see you
hook a pea, perfectly

poised on the tine. I nearly
cheer—*you've done it!*

You will now, surely,
proceed to eat a single pea.

Instead, you remove it
with your other hand,

set it down, begin again.
Late sunlight turns

the tabletop gold,
as you continue singing.

I do not understand,
until, rather suddenly,

I remember that I do.

Upstream

I want to store up the details:
you, drowsy, strawberry

      jam hands in your hair.
      I want to love the details

again. But now you are crying,
and I don't understand.

      Your head on the floor.
      Your face berry bright.

Fourteen months old, you are
marvel after marvel—

      unsteady run over the clover,
      your words taking on shapes

I recognize—*ball, yes,*
water, no. You are a shape

      I don't recognize, winding
      water in an unfamiliar

stream. We are walking
upstream. I hold your hand

      when you let me,
      and when you don't, follow

with my hands open,
palms up as if to say

please or *I don't know,*
hands emptied

yet singing, *here I am,*
here I am, here I am.

Blank Slate

You turn pages of black outlines on white,
dragging fat crayons—water-blue, rose-pink—

over the shapes: sun with a smile, plump
caterpillar, tidy rows of circles and squares.

Lately, though, you are easily bored, ever eager
for movement, arching your back in escape—

and so we go out, into the blue morning, where
late tomatoes are pearls on their slim vines;

where the dill, past its season, forms a dark gold
web; where an unnamed purple flower slips

between the slats of the back fence, as if in greeting.
You don't reach for its bright petals but regard them,

instead, with quiet reverence. There are things
I can't teach you, and things I don't have to.

You are no slate, blank or otherwise—
it's the world and me, awaiting your color.

Light Feast on the Olentangy

The river's edge teems with leafy
groundcover, tiny forest
that steals the sound from our steps.

In its lushness, you stumble silently
in search of stems that glow. Soon
you turn toward me again, petals

starring your chin, stems in your hand
reduced to their centers—and really,
I can understand why you'd want

to consume their color, to get close
to that wild beauty, to know it
in a whole-bodied way. Later

when you lie on the grass, twigs
catching in your curls, I do the same:
watching you watch the branches

etch a web against the pale sky. At least,
this is what I think you see, but perhaps
it's pinecones, or the wind, or something

unknowable in your growing mind.
In my own mind I wonder how we
got here, how once my body carried

yours, but now your wonder
enfolds us both, opens me up each
morning like a field feasting on light.

In Walhalla Ravine,

two ducks paddle upstream:
one emerald, the other soft

bronze, each with a secret violet
on the wing catching late light

over the clear water. Unmoving,
we watch them dive below

the singing surface with a kind
of clumsy elegance, watch them

shake cool droplets from
the waxen gleam of their feathers.

As they depart, you voice your
displeasure, calling them back

to what you know—yourself—
and for that brief moment,

they seem to take note:
an alert, almost kind curve

in the round eye turned toward us,
two creatures on the other side

of the creek, beyond the wild blue
lupine, in a world apart yet shared.

At Darby Creek

How sweet to drink September
air, to walk in mud and green,

you in the carrier on your father's
back. Sweet, how he gifts you

grasses wide as ribbon,
weeds that look like wheat.

Sweet, the way your eyes beam
when I turn toward the pair of you.

How sweet to carry nothing
but cool water for myself,

to walk freely and lightly, yet
beside you still. Sweet, sweet,

through forest or field, how
he knows, and can, and does,

sometimes carry us both.

Shoulder Season

I picture us on a paper map, two dots
connected, gliding from block to block.

Pencil shading for some sky, square
cars tracing wide half-circles around us.

When you fall asleep I keep walking,
even as a coming storm colors the clouds,

even as bulbs of rain pool on the hood
of your stroller, slick the pavement.

I think of how it's been nearly two years
of this grey haze that fades and comes back

again. How I once thought I had to learn
to shake it, or at least to shoulder it in secret.

What I've learned instead is something like
how to walk without watching for rain.

To let go of the maps we draw for ourselves.
To let go of what we think the weather should be.

Wean,
or One Afternoon My Breast Blooms
Bright as a Poppy—

an unshapely copy of itself.
I shiver over the sink,
coaxing milk, pink and viscous,

until slowly, slowly, the pain
unwinds—relief like a fever
breaking. Only later can I trace

the thread of this to your taste,
your changing need for less
from me—this ritual, deeply ours,

once an answer to every need,
receding without warning.
Only then do I grieve and give

thanks, as a mother does,
as light leaves the late
October sky, as the nights

change their shape
to make way for winter,
as they always do.

Meeting Great Grandad After Lockdown

On the way to Indiana, I collect colors:
apples, sunny and round, in piles beneath
bare branches. Leaves burned to ash
on a dark driveway. Bright white turbines,
sharp as toothpicks, spinning against
the blue-grey November sky laid out
like a cloth. In Aunt Leigh's house,
all burgundy and violet, he takes
careful steps through the front door,
white light at the threshold, then settles
into a worn wooden chair. Sixteen months old,
you perch on the seat of his walker and notice
everything: green bill of a John Deere hat,
squared glasses, notches on a silver watch;
his kind eyes and creases, and the places
where he wears his sadness, which you,
by being born, by being here, soften
like morning after a lightless night.

Party Dress

Winter mornings break
from within, windows

black rectangles, dark
eyes opening into

a dark room—your room,
where I feed you after

you've slept three hours
in a row—such progress

that I feel like putting on
records and a party dress—

maybe the forest-green
with its tags still on,

all flounce and gold threads.
Too soon, I'll remember

it's only mid-December—
the tree awaits its trimmings,

we have so many nights
ahead—but for now,

it's enough to carry you
into this cold morning,

donning stretched-out
cotton, curls everywhere,

bodies soft and untamed
as the grey light breaking

over us like a song, both
familiar and brand-new.

At Whetstone Park

Plastic sleds of red, lemon, and blue
shout out their color against the snow,

that thick glimmer packed down hard,
topography of prints and pockets of ice.

You climb each hill, slip down again
in cold air and slicing sunlight

with your pink hat halfway over
your eyes. You fall and rise up,

balance a snowball in your mittens
with such care, only to smash it

to powder with a wild joy,
and for today, I do the same—

unworried under the winter blue
and existing as you do, in the world

with all of yourself, all at once.

Whether Trees Have Bones

I keep a careful list of your lexicon:
single words, mostly nouns—*bird bib*

moon mouse—and miniature phrases
that mirror mine—*thank you bless you*

there you go—until today, when you
watched a leaf spiral from your fingers

and said *I dropped it*—your first
sentence, entirely declarative,

a construct all your own. Every day,
we move deeper into this world

of words bound to become questions
with answers I don't know.

Someday, for instance, you might
ask *whether trees have bones,*

and how will I respond? But today
your small hand warms in mine.

Today we walk the January streets,
stepping over limbs from last night's

storm split open on the sidewalk,
insides rich as marrow.

To My Daughter in the Living Room, Dancing

I've never been good at it—
the dancing or the surrender,

      but you are insistent: curls
      stretched to wild waves

that stream behind your blur
of a body, shrieks clear

      as the cold rain making rivers
      on the window, where surely

the neighbors spot me swaying,
grinning at you below the pane.

      We dance anyway—hands joined
      to twirl with reckless delight,

and I think of how my mother
once said that joy is more

      powerful than sorrow. How
      I didn't believe her. And yet.

Lungs,
or Inside the Winter White We Fold

into a false dark brought on by thick curtains.
You sleep in your crib until you don't, and then

you'll only sleep on me, across me, our bodies
forming a soft X as if to say, this is the place:

this good darkness that somehow feels
like a returning. But I can't see you

stretched over me without seeing
your earlier selves. I can't see you

or me in this inky black, white
noise washing over us like water,

the world not so much blocked out
but right here in this room, in my arms,

in our four lungs layered over each other
like tiny warm animals inside larger ones,

exactly and not at all as we began.

Aubade at Clear Creek

For months I coaxed every ounce,
filled with the fret of not enough.

Now your hunger wanes to a need
for nearness. Now your hair grows

long enough to tame; I pull the teeth
of a wide comb through your curls,

dry them with a damp towel. Dawn
unfurls from black to navy; ice darkens

to pools, revealing a glitter of salt.
I am learning to think less about

what I expect, returning to trails
that emerge from winter, gathering

reeds to bend and braid. As the day
lengthens, you notice our shadows

slanted on the dull grass; I lift
my hands like a dancer and you

do the same: each of us
encircled in new light.

About the Author

Emily Patterson is the author of *So Much Tending Remains* (Kelsay Books, 2022). She received her B.A. in English from Ohio Wesleyan University, where she was awarded the F.L. Hunt Prize and Marie Drennan Prize for Poetry, and her M.A. in Education from Ohio State University. Emily's work has been nominated for the Pushcart Prize and appears in *Rust & Moth, SWWIM Every Day, Mom Egg Review, Minerva Rising Press, Literary Mama, The Sunlight Press,* and elsewhere. She lives with her family in Columbus, Ohio.

www.ingramcontent.com/pod-product-compliance
Lightning Source LLC
Chambersburg PA
CBHW070907100426
42737CB00047B/2979